colour
THERAPY
AN INSPIRATION
NOTEBOOK

Michael O'Mara Books Limited

Illustrated by
Sam Loman

Additional illustrations by
Chellie Carroll & Lizzie Preston

With additional material adapted from www.shutterstock.com

Edited by Tom Asker & Corinne Lucas

Designed by Jack Clucas

Cover design by Angie Allison

Every reasonable effort has been made to acknowledge the authors and
sources of the quotations in this book. Any errors or omissions that may have
occurred are inadvertent, and anyone with any queries is invited to write to the publisher
so that a full acknowledgement may be included in subsequent editions of this work.

First published in Great Britain in 2016 by Michael O'Mara Books Limited,
9 Lion Yard, Tremadoc Road, London SW4 7NQ

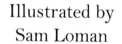

www.mombooks.com
Michael O'Mara Books
@OMaraBooks

A CIP catalogue record for this book is available from the British Library.

ISBN: 978-1-78243-547-1

2 4 6 8 10 9 7 5 3 1

This book was printed in China.

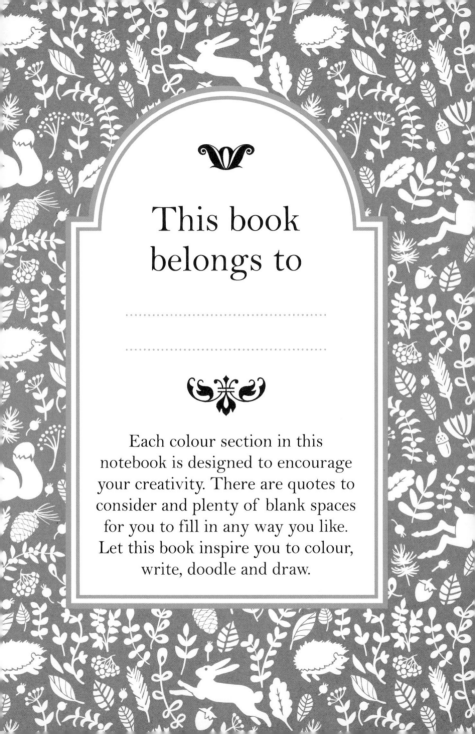

This book belongs to

....

....

Each colour section in this notebook is designed to encourage your creativity. There are quotes to consider and plenty of blank spaces for you to fill in any way you like. Let this book inspire you to colour, write, doodle and draw.

RED

Red is a passionate colour. It can
signify love and desire but it also has
a fiery edge. Heat, danger, aggression:
red is intense, energizing and bold.

'Colour, above all, and perhaps even more
than drawing, is a means of liberation.'

Henri Matisse
The Role and Modalities of Colour (1945)

'Colour is the pulse of a work of art.'

Marc Chagall
Lecture at University of Chicago (1958)

ORANGE

Orange radiates warmth and happiness. It can suggest the comfort of a sizzling fireplace or the rousing inspiration of a sunset. Orange is sensual, provocative and fun.

'The world of reality has its limits; the world of the imagination is boundless.'

Jean-Jacques Rousseau
Emile (1762)

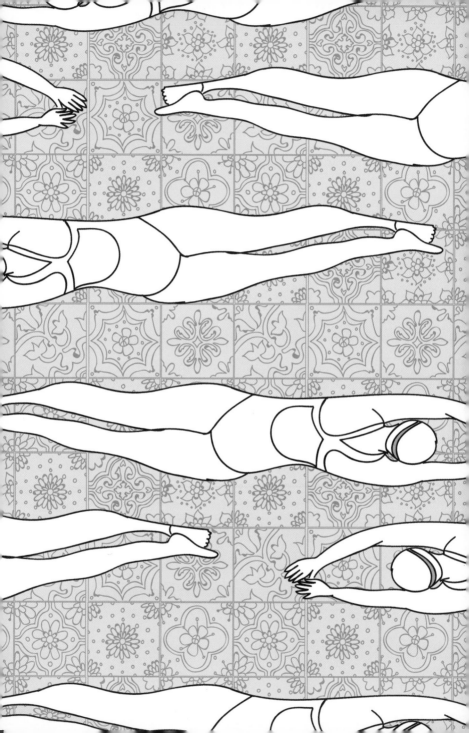

'Art washes away from the soul
the dust of everyday life.'

Pablo Picasso
LIFE Magazine (1964)

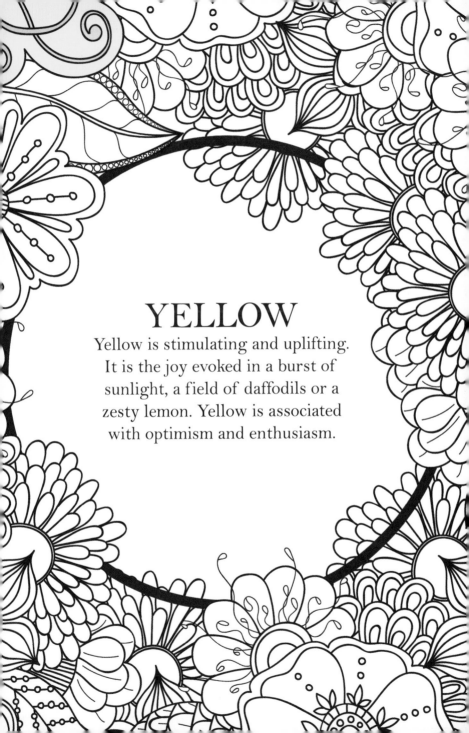

YELLOW

Yellow is stimulating and uplifting. It is the joy evoked in a burst of sunlight, a field of daffodils or a zesty lemon. Yellow is associated with optimism and enthusiasm.

'Let me, O let me bathe my soul
in colours; let me swallow the
sunset and drink the rainbow.'

Kahlil Gibran, letter to Mary Haskell (1908)

'I found I could say things with colour and shapes that I couldn't say any other way - things I had no words for.'

Georgia O'Keeffe
Foreword to an exhibition (1923)

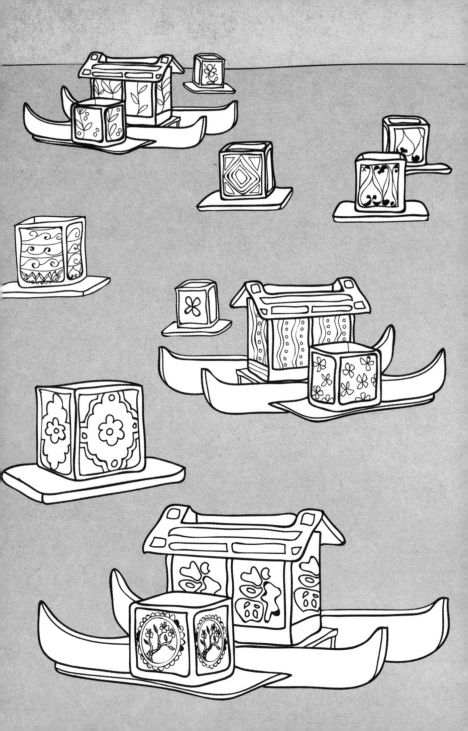

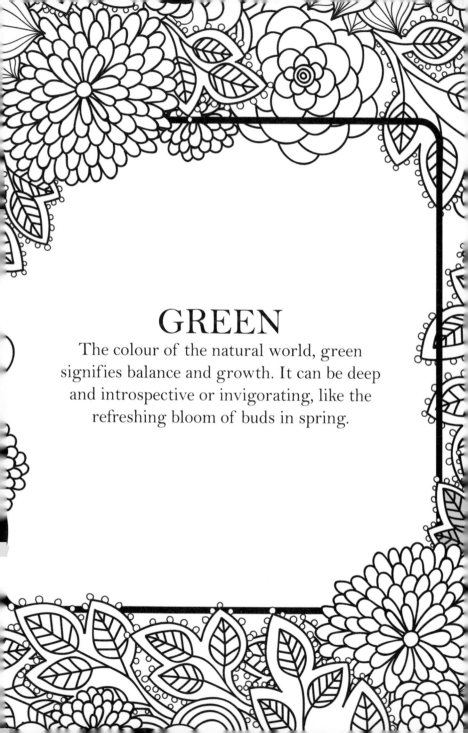

GREEN

The colour of the natural world, green signifies balance and growth. It can be deep and introspective or invigorating, like the refreshing bloom of buds in spring.

'Green is the prime colour of the world,
and that from which its loveliness arises.'

Pedro Calderon de la Barca
La Banda y La Flor (1632)

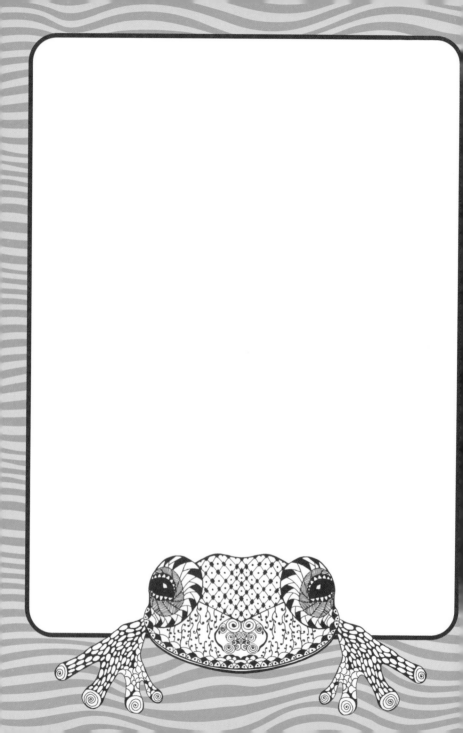

'Colour! What a deep and mysterious
language, the language of dreams.'

Paul Gauguin
From his personal notebook (1896)

BLUE

From the peace of a lake on a still day to the brilliance of a dazzling sky, blue is a colour of great depth. While it can signify order and tranquility, it can also be mysterious and reflective.

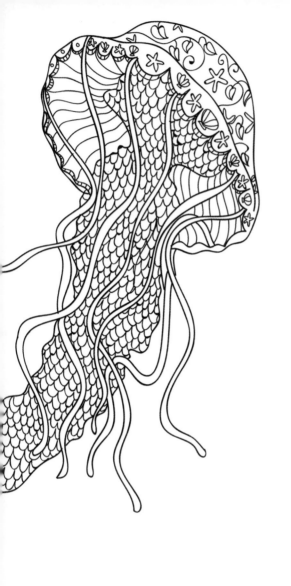

'Colour must be thought, imagined, dreamed.'

Gustave Moreau
Quoted in a student's letter (1891)

'Colours, like features, follow the
changes of the emotions.'

Pablo Picasso
Cahiers d'Art (1935)

INDIGO
& VIOLET

Indigo and violet are luxurious
colours. From delicate flowers and
rich amethysts to bruised, stormy
skies, they can be intensifying,
resplendent and imaginative.

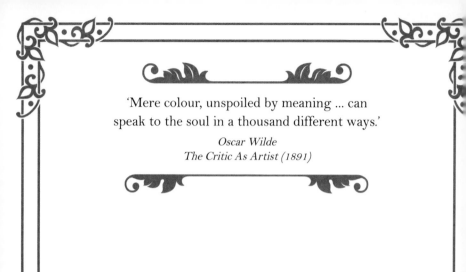

'Mere colour, unspoiled by meaning ... can
speak to the soul in a thousand different ways.'

Oscar Wilde
The Critic As Artist (1891)

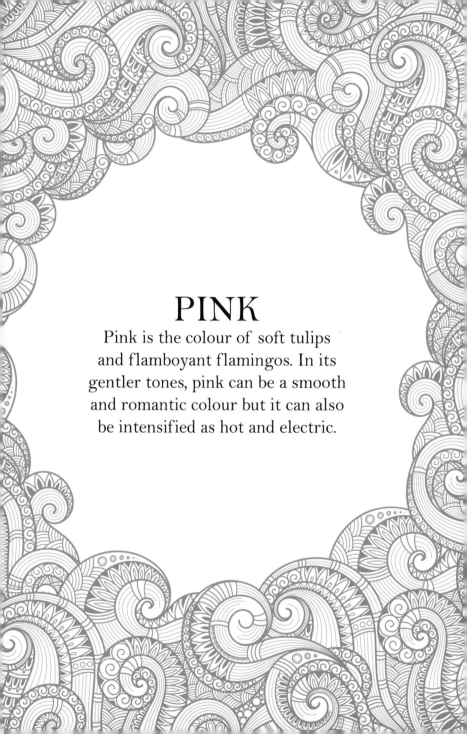

PINK

Pink is the colour of soft tulips
and flamboyant flamingos. In its
gentler tones, pink can be a smooth
and romantic colour but it can also
be intensified as hot and electric.

'Love was a feeling completely bound up
with colour, like thousands of rainbows
superimposed one on top of the other.'

Paulo Coelho, Brida (1990)

- ....
- ....
- ....
- ....
- ....
- ....
- ....
- ....
- ....
- ....
- ....
- ....
- ....
- ....
- ....
- ....

'One can speak poetry just by arranging colours well.'
Vincent van Gogh
Letter to Willemien van Gogh (1888)